CAN YOU SURVIVE

HAIR-RAISING MOUNTAIN ENCOUNTERS?

An Interactive
Wilderness Adventure

by Matt Doeden

CAPSTONE PRESS
a capstone imprint

Published by Capstone Press, an imprint of Capstone
1710 Roe Crest Drive, North Mankato, Minnesota 56003
capstonepub.com

Library of Congress Cataloging-in-Publication Data is available on the Library of
Congress website.
ISBN: 9781666337969 (hardcover)
ISBN: 9781666337976 (paperback)
ISBN: 9781666337983 (ebook PDF)

Summary: Could you survive being lost in the mountains? Imagine facing down a grizzly
bear in the Alaskan wilderness, a mountain lion in the Sierra Madres of Mexico, or a
gorilla in Africa's Virunga Mountains. How far would you be willing to go to save your
own life? Would it work? Flip through these pages to find out!

Editorial Credits
Editor: Mandy Robbins; Designer: Heidi Thompson; Media Researchers: Jo Miller and
Pam Mitsakos; Production Specialist: Tori Abraham

Image Credits
Alamy: robertharding, 16; Getty Images: skiserge1, 103; Shutterstock: Alex Bordeline,
47, AlexZaitsev, design element, throughout, Daniel Grima Adventure, 22, David Havel,
91, Denys.Kutsevalov, 73, dylancr27, 33, Ernie Cooper, 68, erwinf., 88, Evgeniyqw,
Cover, Jay Yuan, 27, JONATHAN PLEDGER, 93, Maciej Czekajewski, 50, Nataly
Reinch, 84, Nathan A Shepard, 56, Olga Danylenko, 100, 112, Ondrej Prosicky, 52, Petr
Muckstein, 81, Shcherbyna Nataliia, 13, stacyarturogi, 63, Szczepan Klejbuk, 30, valiant.
skies, 37

TABLE OF CONTENTS

FACING MOUNTAIN DANGERS!

YOU are deep in a majestic mountain wilderness. You're surrounded by beauty—and danger. Rockslides and avalanches are constant threats. Deadly wildlife—including bears, wolves, and mountain lions—could lurk at every turn.

What will you do when you come face-to-face with a deadly mountain creature? Will you fight? Will you run? Do you have what it takes to survive a dangerous mountain wildlife encounter? YOU CHOOSE which paths to take. Your choices will guide the story and decide—will you live or die?

• Turn the page to begin your adventure.

CHAPTER 1

INTO THE MOUNTAINS

There's nothing quite like the mountains. You take a deep breath, inhaling the fresh smell of mountain air. The trees, the rocks, the calm and quiet—there's just nowhere you'd rather be. Out here, it's just you and nature.

But even as you enjoy the scenery and the setting, you know that it's not entirely the peaceful place it seems to be.

• Turn the page.

The mountains can be as harsh as they are beautiful, and the wildlife here has adapted to survive in these conditions. In a place where resources can be scarce, some of the animals here will do anything for a meal. And if you find yourself in the wrong place at the wrong time, that could be you.

So even as you hike through the wilderness, you keep your eyes and ears open. Every sound, from the wind through the trees to a birdcall, gets your complete attention. Predators lurk out here. You can never let your guard down.

A gust of wind blows across your face. You move carefully over the uneven ground. Suddenly, you have the unmistakable feeling that you're being watched. Something is out there, and it's tracking your every move.

You turn and look all around you. High mountain peaks reach up toward the bright blue sky. Shadowy forests surround you.

The sound of a snapping branch makes the hairs on your arm stand on end. Something is coming your way. What is it? You don't know. But you prepare yourself to act. It's beautiful out here in the mountain wilderness, but still, you know you must be ready for anything.

- To explore Alaska's Denali National Park and Preserve, turn to page 11.
- To take a trip to Mexico's Sierra Madre mountain range, turn to page 45.
- To brave the mountains of Virunga National Park in the Congo, turn to page 71.

CHAPTER 2

SURVIVING DENALI

"Wow, is this the perfect spot or what?" Kwan says, gazing toward the towering peaks of Alaska's Denali National Park and Preserve. The snowcapped mountains stand out against a bright blue sky. You think you spy a hint of pink in the west, as the sun begins to dip lower in the sky. The wind through the trees sounds like nature's whispering some secret language. The first day of your backpacking adventure has been just like you dreamed it would be.

• Turn the page.

You smile and nod. "Yeah, it's pretty great. I've dreamed of backpacking out here since I was little. I'm so glad you came with me."

Kwan has been your best friend since first grade. There is no one you'd rather share this adventure with.

"Now make yourself useful and find us some more dry wood," you joke. "This fire isn't going to feed itself."

It's late afternoon, and the shadows of Denali are getting long. You've pitched your tent in a small clearing in the trees. You're both ready to relax by a fire after a long day of climbing and hiking.

Kwan comes with an armful of wood just as you get a small fire going. You arrange some small logs onto the fire in a pyramid. Soon, you've got a roaring blaze going.

• Turn the page.

With plans to be up here for a week, you expect to forage for some of your food. Your backpack is stocked with trail mix, jerky, and more. Tonight, however, you've got a treat in mind—hot dogs. You each grab a small stick, jab a hot dog onto the end, and hold them over the flames. The smell is amazing.

"There's nothing like cooking over a fire after a hard day of hiking," you say.

Kwan agrees. You can tell he's hungry when you hear his stomach growling.

You laugh. "Man, you *are* hungry," you say.

He gives you a funny look. "What are you talking about? That was your stomach, not mine."

Then you hear the sound again. It's a deep growling noise. But it's not coming from your stomach—or Kwan's. It's coming from a dense patch of forest beyond the clearing.

By instinct, you scramble to your feet. You peer into the trees and see a shape. A big shape.

"Grizzly bear," you whisper.

Kwan sees it too. "Not just one," he says, pointing. "Look over there."

A lone grizzly bear would probably leave you alone. But this is a mother bear with two cubs. The cubs have wandered into the clearing, just a stone's throw from your camp. The smell of the hot dogs probably drew them in.

There's one thing you know about bears. Nothing is more dangerous than a mother with her cubs. She will do anything to protect her offspring. With the cubs so close to you, you are in a very dangerous position. You have bear spray in your backpack, but it's out of reach in the tent. It won't do you any good here.

• Turn the page.

"Throw them the hot dogs," Kwan says. "Then we can make a run for it."

You're not sure feeding the bears is a great idea. But you have to do something.

- To throw the hot dogs, go to page 17.
- To shout at the bears to go away, turn to page 19.

In your panic, you can't think of a better idea. The smell of the food probably brought the bears to the clearing. So you pluck the hot dogs off of the sticks and throw them as far as you can toward the family of bears. Hoping that's enough to distract them, you turn and dart for the other side of the clearing. Kwan isn't quite as fast as you are. He lags a few steps behind you.

You realize quickly that your plan didn't work. The mother bear either didn't notice the food or doesn't care. Bears are predators, and their instinct is to chase. Branches snap as the mother grizzly begins to charge. As you run, you glance over your shoulder. She's coming right at you. It's amazing how fast such a large animal can be. You can't outrun her. You need to find a safe place—and quickly!

• Turn the page.

You run full-speed into the woods. Branches slap you in the face, but you barely feel them. Kwan is right be hind you. You can hear the bear getting closer by the second.

A tall spruce tree rises in front of you. Off to the side, a group of boulders rise up out of the ground.

- To run for the boulders, turn to page 22.
- To climb the tree, turn to page 33.

You think you read somewhere that trying to scare some predators is actually smarter than running from them. The mother bear is staring at you. You don't have much time to act. You rise to your feet, spreading your arms and legs wide to look as big as you possibly can.

"Get out of here!" you shout. "GO!"

The cubs dart back into the safety of the trees. The mother stares at you a moment longer. You fear that she could charge at any moment. So you shout some more. You wave your arms around. Finally, she decides that you aren't worth the trouble. She turns and disappears into the shadows.

You and Kwan are both shaking. After a minute, Kwan finally speaks. "Let's eat these hot dogs now, before she changes her mind."

• Turn the page.

He's right. The smell of cooking meat out here could draw her back or lure other predators. You both wolf down your hot dogs in less than a minute. You barely even taste them in your rush. Then you grab your bear spray and stack more wood onto the fire. A good roaring blaze will make you feel safer tonight.

You sleep in shifts, with one of you keeping watch and tending the fire all night. Sunrise is a big relief. You pack up your things and get ready to continue your adventure.

The mountain air is crisp and cool. You hike along a small stream, taking in the sights and sounds.

Suddenly, Kwan stops and points. "What's that?"

Alongside the stream, a small, dark-furred animal lies on the ground. It appears to be wounded. Dried blood mats the fur on one of its legs.

"Wolverine," you whisper. "I wonder what happened to it."

You take out your phone and snap a few photos.

"Get closer," Kwan says. "How often do you get to photograph a wild wolverine?"

• To keep your distance, turn to page 29.
• To get a closer look, turn to page 35.

21

Bears can climb trees—that won't save you. "This way," you shout back to Kwan. You turn hard to the right. There's a large crack where two boulders lean against each other. You jam your body into the space, wedging yourself in as deep as you can. Kwan follows you in, and the bear is right behind.

The crack is too small for her to fit inside. She takes a mighty swipe with her front paw. She can reach just far enough that her front claws rake across Kwan's left leg. He shouts out in pain.

After a few moments, the bear retreats. You wait, huddled in the crack, for a few minutes more, making sure she's gone.

When you come out, you see the damage. Kwan's leg is badly hurt. Long, deep gashes run down his calf. He's losing blood. You remove your sweatshirt and wrap it tightly around his upper leg to slow the bleeding. Then you let Kwan lean on you as he carefully hobbles back to the clearing. There are no longer any bears in sight.

• Turn the page.

"It's bad," Kwan says with a grimace. "There's no way I can hike out of here."

You nod. The sun is low in the sky. You have an hour or so of daylight left. You're going to need to go for help. Leaving now would mean hiking in the dark. But waiting until morning is risky too. Kwan has lost a lot of blood. Can he hold out that long?

You help Kwan back to camp and get him comfortable. Neither choice you have is great. But you have to decide, and soon.

• To go for help now, go to page 25.
• To wait until morning, turn to page 27.

You shake your head, your mind made up. "You need help fast. I'm going now."

You grab your backpack, check on Kwan one last time, and head out. You hand him the can of bear spray. You'd feel better keeping it. But if the bear does return, it may be his only defense. "Just hold on, Kwan," you tell him. "I'll be back with help as fast as I can."

As the sun dips lower in the sky, the temperature drops. You keep a quick pace, heading for the nearest road through the park.

Night falls over Denali. The sky is filled with stars. It would be beautiful if you had the time to admire the view. But you press on, moving as quickly as you dare in the darkness.

A long, ghostly howl stops you in your tracks.

• Turn the page.

"Wolf," you whisper to yourself. It's hard to tell how far away the sound was. But it sounded close enough to make you nervous.

Another howl, then another. Your heartbeat races. This isn't a lone wolf. It's a pack. And that's dangerous. You really, really wish you had your bear spray right now.

A few minutes later, you come upon a clearing. In the moonlight, you see the shapes. Wolves. At least six of them. Their eyes seem to glow. And they're all locked on you.

You need to act now, before they decide that you look like dinner. Should you make yourself look like a threat? Or should you get out of here as fast as your feet can carry you?

• To try to intimidate the pack, turn to page 31.
• To run into the trees, turn to page 42.

"It's too late to go out for help now," you tell Kwan. "I'll go for help as soon as it's daylight."

You spend the night taking care of him, dressing his wounds, making sure he's warm and has plenty to drink. He's in a lot of pain, but his life doesn't seem to be in any danger. You give him some ibuprofen that you had packed in case you got a headache.

• Turn the page.

At sunrise, you head out. It's a long hike to the nearest road. It's almost noon by the time you reach it and flag down a park ranger making her morning rounds.

"I need help," you call out. You explain what happened and where your friend is.

The ranger acts quickly. Her truck is designed to handle off-road driving, so you hop in and guide her back to Kwan.

"Don't worry," she assures you. "I'll call for a medical evacuation just as soon as I have his coordinates. Everything will be okay."

• Turn to page 41.

Wolverines are ferocious creatures. A wounded one might still do all kinds of damage with its sharp claws and teeth. "No, I think this is close enough," you say with a chuckle. You take a few more photos, then move along. "I just hope it's okay. Looks like something took a chunk out of its leg."

You spend the next few days above the tree line, climbing, hiking, and camping. Then you head back down into the forest. It's time to go home.

The two of you are happily walking and talking. You're not paying much attention, when you come around a bend to a shocking surprise. There, in front of you, stands an enormous moose, complete with a set of huge antlers. You're so close, you can feel its hot, wet breath.

• Turn the page.

Your sudden appearance startles the moose.
It's about to charge!

- To turn around and run the other way, turn to page 38.
- To dive into some bushes off to the side, turn to page 39.

Wolves are predators. They're born to chase. This pack hasn't decided yet what to do with you, but if you run you know their instinct to chase will kick in. No, that's not the answer. Your only hope is to convince the wolves that attacking you isn't worth the effort.

So you stand tall. You spread your arms out. And you shout at them at the top of your lungs.

The wolves hesitate. Several of them take a few steps backward. You shout again. Finally, one of them turns and trots off in the other direction. The rest follow.

You let out a deep breath and put your head in your hands. "That was intense," you mumble to yourself.

• Turn the page.

After taking a moment to calm yourself, you continue on your way. After about an hour, you come across a small path—just two dirt ruts in the ground. You follow it until you find a small ranger station. And you're in luck—the light is on! Someone is working late.

A surprised park ranger opens the door when you pound on it. "Help," you say breathlessly. "My friend is hurt—bear attack."

The park ranger reacts quickly. She grabs a first-aid kit and hurries outside. "Come on, I've got a four-wheeler. Take me to your friend. I'll radio for medical evacuation."

• Turn to page 41.

You lunge for the tree. "Come on!" you shout to Kwan. You scramble up the branches, trying to get as high as you can. Kwan is right behind you.

• Turn the page.

You pull yourself up out of reach with just a second to spare. The bear rises up on her hind legs, but she can't quite reach you. You stare down at her sharp teeth as she roars up at you.

It worked! For a moment, you think that all you'll have to do is wait up here until she gives up and wanders away. But your relief is short-lived. You realize your mistake when the bear sinks her front claws into the trunk of the spruce and begins to haul herself up.

Bears are excellent climbers.

You're trapped. There's nowhere to go. No way to fight back. Your dream adventure is over, and it's not going to be a happy ending.

THE END

To follow another path, turn to page 9.
To learn more about mountain survival, turn to page 99.

You know wolverines are ferocious creatures. But this one is wounded. How dangerous could it be? The wolverine lies still as you creep closer. It's alive—you can see it breathing. You step a little closer and lift your phone. As you take the picture, your phone makes a loud clicking shutter sound. Suddenly, the startled wolverine springs to life. The little animal is all claws and teeth as it lunges at you. Now you know just what a wolverine can do. Unfortunately, you had to learn the hard way.

The attack lasts only a few seconds. But by the time the animal limps off into the woods, the damage is done. You've got long, deep scratches on your arms and chest.

Kwan rushes to your side. He wraps the wounds to stop the bleeding.

• Turn the page.

"We need to get you to a hospital," he says.

Walking is incredibly painful. But you have no choice. With your arm around Kwan's shoulder, you start the long hike back to civilization. You wanted a good photo of a wolverine. Instead, you'll have scars to remind you of the terrifying encounter for the rest of your life.

THE END

To follow another path, turn to page 9.
To learn more about mountain survival, turn to page 99.

You have no time to think. So you do the first thing that comes to mind. You turn and run.

Kwan, standing behind you, doesn't react as quickly. As you turn, you barrel straight into him. Both of you fall to the ground in a heap.

That's not a good place to be. The charging moose lowers its head, slamming its antlers into your body. The animal keeps running, trampling you with its hooves in the process.

Your world goes dark. You survived encounters with some of Denali's most dangerous predators. Who would have thought a moose would have been the one to bring your adventure to such a tragic end?

THE END

To follow another path, turn to page 9.
To learn more about mountain survival, turn to page 99.

The moose is about to charge, and running won't do you a bit of good. In one swift motion, you grab Kwan's arm. You drag him with you as you dive off to the side into some thick bushes.

Sharp branches claw at your face and body, but it's a price well worth paying. The startled moose darts off, the sound of its heavy steps quickly fading into the forest.

• Turn the page.

"Whoa, that was close," Kwan says as the two of you pick yourselves up and brush off.

Your heart is racing, but you can't help but laugh. All this time you've been worried about bears and wolverines. And it was a moose that almost did you in!

You shake your head. "I guess you just never know what to expect in the wilderness. Come on, let's keep moving. It's been a great time. But I'm ready for a hot shower and a warm bed."

THE END

To follow another path, turn to page 9.
To learn more about mountain survival, turn to page 99.

Within half an hour, you're back at your campsite. Kwan's breathing is shallow. But he's awake. He gives you a smile as you rush to his side. "What took you so long?" he asks.

"I think you'll be just fine," the ranger says, as she dresses Kwan's wounds. "A helicopter is on its way to take you to the hospital. You're lucky. Not everyone comes face-to-face with a grizzly bear and lives to tell the tale."

THE END

To follow another path, turn to page 9.
To learn more about mountain survival, turn to page 99.

Panic wells up inside you. Fear makes you act foolishly. You turn and run as fast as you can toward the trees. But like dogs, wolves can't resist a chase. The minute you run, you become prey in their eyes.

You have no chance. They're much, much faster than you are. Maybe you could fight off a single wolf. But not six of them. They're too fast, too strong, and too hungry. And they're used to working as a team. They come at you from all sides, teeth gnashing.

Kwan was counting on you, and you let him down. And now you're going to pay a very steep price. There's a good chance he will too.

THE END

To follow another path, turn to page 9.
To learn more about mountain survival, turn to page 99.

CHAPTER 3

A TRIP INTO THE SIERRA MADRES

The sun shines brightly overhead as you make your way along a rugged trail. The slopes of Mexico's beautiful Sierra Madre mountain range rise up all around you. The trail leads through forests of pine and oak along a deep canyon that is surrounded by mountain peaks.

• Turn the page.

It's been a peaceful hike since you left your family back at your campsite this morning. They were all exhausted from a day of hiking yesterday. Nobody was up for another all-day trek. So you grabbed your backpack and headed out on your own, promising to return by dinnertime.

You don't mind being by yourself. In fact, it's what you've really been looking forward to about this trip. You love your family, but there's something about being alone with nature that just makes you feel alive. All the worries of the world back home seem to melt away when it's just you and the mountains.

Your mind wanders as you walk, taking in the scenery and munching on a strip of beef jerky. Suddenly, you feel a chill go down your spine. You have a strong sense that you're being watched.

You spin around, scanning the trees behind you. There's nothing but trail there.

"Hmmm," you mutter to yourself. You keep watching for a moment. You just can't shake the feeling that you're not alone. But you don't see anyone else here, so you continue on your way.

• Turn the page.

A minute later, you hear something—the rustling of leaves. Once again, you turn around. This time, you're not alone. Just a stone's throw behind you, is a large cougar—also known as a mountain lion. Its gaze is locked on you.

The big cat moves slowly toward you, opening its mouth to show its large, sharp teeth. You know from reading that mountain lions are ambush predators. They look for unsuspecting prey. That could give you an advantage here. The cat isn't going to surprise you, and it knows it.

"Easy now," you say with a quiver in your voice. You extend your arm. "Easy."

The mountain lion continues to walk slowly toward you. It moves silently on its large paws—a predator ready to strike.

You're alone and exposed, with nowhere to run. If the big cat pounces, there's nothing you can do to save yourself.

It's time to act. You could try to retreat, or you could see if food might distract the mountain lion.

- To throw your beef jerky to distract the big cat, turn to page 50.
- To slowly back away, turn to page 52.

A mountain lion would only approach you for one reason—it's hungry. So you hurl your strip of beef jerky right at the animal. At first, your movement seems to startle the lion. It steps back. But the smell of the jerky quickly gets its attention. It leans over, sniffs at the jerky, and scarfs it down in one big gulp. While it does this, you don't waste any time. You reach inside your pack and grab a few more strips. You throw those as well, hoping it will be enough to satisfy the animal. If nothing else, it will buy you some time.

Your plan seems to work. The mountain lion lays down as it munches on the snack. With it distracted, you quickly move along the trail, putting as much distance between it and you as you can.

After a few minutes, you stop to take stock of your situation. Your close encounter has you feeling uneasy. You have a powerful urge to get back to your campsite and your family. But this is a one-way trail. The only way back is the way you came.

- To continue hiking on the trail, turn to page 54.
- To wait a few minutes, then go back, turn to page 60.

"Scram!" you call out to the mountain lion, as you slowly back away. "Get out of here!"

You keep your gaze locked on the cat as you move. Mountain lions like the element of surprise. As long as it knows you're watching, it will be careful.

You continue to back away for a minute or two, as the mountain lion keeps pace. Suddenly, the mountains seem quiet. The only sounds are your footsteps and the occasional snarl from the big cat. You never take your eyes off your stalker. You don't want to give it even the smallest opening to strike.

After a minute, the mountain lion stops. It watches you for a few seconds more, then leaps off of the trail into the forest. It must have decided to look for easier prey. You let out a deep breath.

• Turn to page 54.

You know one thing for sure—rattlesnakes can't climb rocks. You grab hold and pull yourself up, scaling the rock as quickly as you can. After a few moments, you look down. Sure enough, a large snake sits coiled under one of the boulders below. It shakes its trademark rattle—a sure sign that the snake feels threatened and is ready to strike.

"Sheesh," you mutter. "First a mountain lion, now a rattlesnake?" Maybe heading out for a hike by yourself wasn't the best idea after all.

After you calm yourself, you continue your climb. Boulders stack up on top of each other, allowing you to scramble up easily. You work your way up to a large rocky ledge. But as you reach to pull yourself up, you spot a small, dark shape right where you're about to put your hand. It's a scorpion!

- To quickly pull your hand away, turn to page 66.
- To ignore the scorpion and complete your climb, turn to page 68.

That rattle sends you into a panic. So you do the first thing you think of. You run!

It may be instinct, but it was a bad decision. Because when you turn to run, you charge directly at the snake! The startled creature strikes, sinking its long fangs into your left leg. The bite lasts only a second or two, but you know that's enough. The snake's deadly venom is surely coursing through your veins already.

You run back to the path, then collapse onto the ground. The bite hurts, but it's not too bad. You roll up your pant leg to see that the wound is already swelling up. You know that rattlesnake bites are rarely deadly if treated. The effects should be minor. But already you're feeling dizzy and ill. Your stomach is cramping. You feel like you might throw up.

You shake your head. "Something isn't right," you say to yourself. The venom shouldn't be having these effects so quickly . . . unless you're allergic. And if that's the case, your life is in grave danger.

You stand up, but immediately feel dizzy. You're afraid you might faint. How can you hike back to camp feeling like this? Maybe you should rest for awhile before you head back.

• To try to make it back to camp, turn to page 62.
• To rest here, turn to page 65.

There's only one way back to your family. You have to go back the way you came. Under the shade of a tree, you wait 15 minutes. The mountain lion should have moved on by now . . . right?

You try to walk as quietly as you can on the way back, just in case the mountain lion is still nearby. Your heart races as you come to the spot where you saw it. But there's nothing here. The animal is gone.

You pick up the pace, eager to get back.

That's when you hear it. The low, rumbling growl. You spin to your left, just in time to see a flash of light brown fur and gleaming teeth.

When you fed the mountain lion your jerky, you showed it that you were a source of food. So you can hardly blame it for coming back for more. You just wish it didn't have you in mind this time around.

THE END

To follow another path, turn to page 9.
To learn more about mountain survival, turn to page 99.

If this is an allergy to the venom, you need to move quickly. You ignore the pain and collect your thoughts. All you can do is try. You head back down the trail for camp. It's at least a 45-minute hike. You move as fast as you can.

At one point, you have to stop to throw up. It would be so easy just to lay down and rest. But that would be a death sentence. You have to keep going. Fifteen minutes pass. Twenty. You keep stumbling down the path.

You're feeling worse and worse. Just when you think you'll never make it, you hear something . . . voices. Two people appear from around a bend—a young man and woman. They're wearing park ranger uniforms! It's just the lucky break you've been needing. As soon as they see you, they can tell you're in trouble. They rush to your side and bear most of your weight.

"Come with us," says the young woman. "Our ranger station is just a few minutes up the trail. We have a first-aid kit with medicine."

• Turn the page.

You feel like you're about to pass out, but you manage to make it to the station just in time. The woman, Selena, digs out a dose of epinephrine—a medicine that treats severe allergic reactions. She quickly gives you the drug. Within minutes, you're feeling better.

"I think you're going to make it," says Peter, the young man. "You're lucky we found you when we did. Now come on, let's get you back to your campsite. You'll need to find a hospital for antivenom."

You can't thank Selena and Peter enough. They saved your life. And now you've got an amazing story of survival to tell all your friends when you get back home.

THE END

To follow another path, turn to page 9.
To learn more about mountain survival, turn to page 99.

You quickly sit back down before you faint. Your heart is racing. Your thoughts feel fuzzy and confused.

You're definitely having an allergic reaction. Your immune system is reacting to the venom. Your body is starting to shut down.

"HELP!" you shout. Maybe there are other hikers out here who can hear you. "Anyone! Help me!"

But no one answers. Your symptoms are getting worse by the minute. Your skin breaks out in an itchy rash. Your leg is swelling more and more. And your thoughts grow fuzzier and fuzzier.

You lie down. You're so tired. You just need to close your eyes for a moment. It's a shame you won't open them again.

THE END

To follow another path, turn to page 9.
To learn more about mountain survival, turn to page 99.

"Ahhhhh!" you scream. Mountain lions, rattlesnakes, and now a scorpion. For the third time today, you're terrified.

Instinctively, you jerk your hand away to avoid a painful sting. But the sudden movement throws you off-balance. Your body weight shifts back, and your other hand loses its grip with the rock wall.

That's a bad thing. With both hands off the rock face, you tumble backward and begin to fall. It's not a long drop—maybe 15 feet. But you land hard on the jagged boulders below. You hear bones in your back snap and pop as you crash down. Pain surges through your body.

As you tumble toward flat ground, you realize that you can't feel your legs. You're paralyzed! And now you're here, all alone. You can't stand up. All you can do is call for help.

Maybe someone will hear you. Maybe someone will help. Or maybe this was the mistake that will cost you your life.

THE END

To follow another path, turn to page 9.
To learn more about mountain survival, turn to page 99.

After a quick surge of terror, you realize that the scorpion is no danger to you. It's just a little one, and it quickly scurries away as soon as your hand comes near it. It doesn't want to sting you. It just wants to be safe. You pull yourself up onto the ledge, laughing at your own reaction. After surviving a mountain lion encounter and a close call with a rattlesnake, you almost panicked over a little harmless scorpion.

You sit down on the ledge to rest and take in the scenery. It's a beautiful spot. Despite all of your heart-stopping encounters, you feel relaxed and recharged. You spend the next few hours exploring and climbing. It's just the kind of adventure you've been needing.

When you head back to camp, your family is there waiting for you. You give them a big grin, excited to tell them about your adventures and all your close encounters with the local wildlife. And you can't wait to go explore more tomorrow.

THE END

To follow another path, turn to page 9.
To learn more about mountain survival, turn to page 99.

CHAPTER 4

A CONGO ADVENTURE

"These little pests just won't leave me alone!" says Anya, slapping her forehead. She wipes a drop of blood from her hand, scowling.

You sigh. It's your third day in the Congo's Virunga Mountains. Swarms of bloodthirsty mosquitoes have plagued you since you got here. There are four people in your research group, but the mosquitoes seem to like Anya the most. Her arms are covered in welts, even though she soaks herself in bug spray several times each day.

• Turn the page.

"Everybody grab your gear, we're going to cover some ground today," Tina commands. She is in charge of your group. Tina is a graduate student studying insect life in the Congo. You, Anya, and Samir are college juniors, chosen by your university's biology department to help her collect and catalog insects from this remote region. For you, it's the trip of a lifetime.

The Virunga Mountains are a series of volcanic peaks that rise up out of the rain forest in the eastern part of the Congo. The word *virunga* actually comes from the word volcanoes in Kinyarwanda, a local language. As you sling your backpack over your shoulder, you look up at the towering peaks. You've never been anywhere like this. It feels like you're a million miles from home.

• Turn the page.

The four of you trek into the jungle, climbing a gradual slope toward one of the tree-covered mountains. Along the way, you turn over dead logs, look under rocks, and dig in the dirt as you search for different species of insects. The highlight of your day is spotting a bright orange butterfly called a white-barred acraea.

Along the base of the mountain, the four of you spread out. You're busy munching on a protein bar and looking under a log for rare bugs when you hear a deep, loud grunt. It's followed by the rustling of leaves.

You look up to a sight that takes your breath away. There, not far from you, is a rare mountain gorilla. It's staring at you through the trees.

The huge primate takes a few steps toward you. It walks mostly on its legs, but also uses its arms to scoot along the forest floor. You can see a patch of silver on its sides and back. It's a male, and you can tell it's not sure what to make of you being in its territory. The gorilla rises up on its legs and loudly beats its chest. You know from research that it's a display of power. The gorilla is letting you know that he's in charge here.

Your heart is racing. The gorilla is so close now that you're pretty sure you smell it. The powerful beast could crush you if it decides to attack. You're in incredible danger. You're not sure if your teammates are close enough to hear you. Should you call for help or just curl up into a ball and hope the gorilla goes away?

• To yell for help, turn to page 76.
• To curl up into a ball and hope the gorilla goes away, turn to page 77.

In a panic, you shout at the top of your lungs. "Help! Somebody help!"

The sudden noise seems to startle the gorilla. For a moment, it hesitates. It even backs away half a step. But then it fixes its gaze on you and charges. For such a huge animal, it moves with incredible grace and speed.

It stops, hovering right in front of you. You can feel its hot breath on your face. You search your brain for ideas. Maybe giving the gorilla a treat will calm the animal. Or should you try to scare him away?

- To hold out the energy bar to the gorilla, turn to page 78.
- To stand up and try to make yourself look like a threat, turn to page 88.

You aren't prey to this gorilla. It's not interested in eating you. The only thing he cares about is whether you are a threat to him or his troop. Your best chance is to show it that you're not a threat. You calmly curl up into a ball, tucking in your arms and legs tightly. You make yourself look small. You turn your head away from the gorilla, in case it might view eye contact as a threat.

You can hear the huge animal grunting and breathing as you hold the position. It spends a few moments looking at you. Then, as suddenly as it appeared, it disappears into the forest. Just to be safe, you hold the position for a few minutes longer. Finally, you let out a deep breath, knowing that you just survived an incredibly rare wildlife encounter.

• Turn to page 80.

The giant animal towers over you. You turn your head away and do the only thing that makes sense to you. You hold out the protein bar you've been eating.

The gorilla leans in, sniffing at the bar. After a long, terrifying moment, he plucks the bar out of your hand and eats it. Then he does the most surprising thing you can imagine. He plops down next to you and begins grooming your hair.

For a moment, you're frozen in shock and fear. But then you realize that the gorilla isn't going to hurt you. He's treating you like another ape . . . which you suppose is exactly what you are. Carefully, you reach into your backpack and grab another protein bar. You unwrap it and hold it out. The gorilla eagerly takes the bar and eats it in two big bites.

The two of you spend a few more minutes sitting side by side. It's an amazing experience. You realize that this is no mere animal. It's a thinking being. Not human . . . but not really so different from you.

Without warning, your new friend gets up and trots off into the forest. You're left staring into the thick trees, barely able to believe what just happened.

THE END

To follow another path, turn to page 9.
To learn more about mountain survival, turn to page 99.

Your friends can barely believe your story about the gorilla. In fact, you're pretty sure Samir thinks you're lying. "Keep your eyes open for friendly gorillas, everyone," he announces. "And if you see one, ask it if it's seen any interesting bugs lately."

Anya pats your arm. "Ignore him," she says. "Now come on. Tina says there's a river not far from here. She wants to see if there are any interesting water insects there."

You make your way through the forest to a wide river. The trees open up here to flat, muddy riverbanks. Tina wastes no time. She starts digging in the mud, looking for insect treasures.

You and Samir head down to the riverbank. "Check out that fallen tree over there," Samir says.

The uprooted tree lies in a shallow section of river, just beyond the bank. You roll up your pants and wade in to check it out. All kinds of bugs could be making the rotting wood their home.

• Turn the page.

As you near the tree, you notice some strange ripples in the water. Something seems to be moving. It looks like the top of a large rock.

"What's that?" you ask.

Samir takes a quick look and shrugs. "Probably just some sort of fish. Come on, let's keep going."

It doesn't look like a fish. Maybe you should keep your distance. But if you avoided everything out here that could be dangerous, you'd never get any work done.

- To grab Samir and head back to the riverbank, go to page 83.
- To ignore the ripples and continue on, turn to page 90.

You don't take your eyes off the water. "Samir," you say in a cracking voice. "That's no fish. Look!"

Now you can make out a shape just below the water. A very large shape, headed right for you. It's a hippo. They're incredibly territorial and aggressive. You do not want to be on the wrong end of a hippo attack.

You grab Samir by the arm and pull. He resists for a moment. Then he realizes the danger you're both in. The two of you slosh back to shore as fast as you can. You pull yourselves up onto the muddy bank and look back. Two eyes peer at you from just above the water's surface. To your relief, the hippo turns and sinks back below the water.

"Phew," you say. Your heart is racing. Samir is shaking.

• Turn the page.

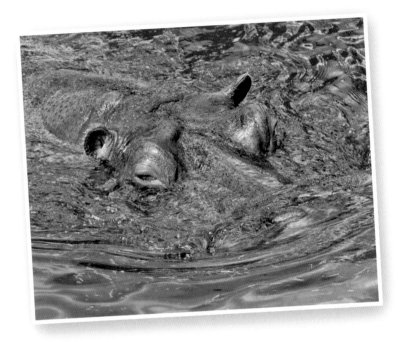

Tina and Anya rush over to see what all the commotion was about. Still short of breath, all the explanation you can offer is, "Hippo."

That's all anyone needs to hear. You grab your gear and head for higher ground, eager to get away from the water's edge.

The four of you chat as you walk through the forest. At the base of the mountain, an open, grassy area stretches out before you.

"Look at that," Tina says with a gasp. Then you see it. About a dozen elephants graze near the base of the mountain.

Anya squeals in delight. She's mentioned to you before how much she loves elephants. "Come on, let's get a closer look," she says, tugging on your arm.

You don't move. "Are you sure that's a good idea, Anya? Look at the size of them."

She rolls her eyes. "Elephants are social, intelligent animals. And they are plant eaters. Come on, it will be fine."

• To go with Anya, turn to page 86.
• To keep your distance, turn to page 92.

You shrug your shoulders and follow Anya as she heads out across the open grassland. Samir and Tina stay behind. "Be careful, please," Tina calls out.

Anya gives her a wave. "We'll be fine."

As you move closer, several of the elephants take notice of you. One of the largest turns to face you. She puffs her big ears out and sways back and forth.

"Umm, Anya," you say. "I'm not sure she's very happy about us being here."

Anya nods. "Yeah, the ears are a warning. We probably shouldn't get any closer."

Anya pulls out her camera and starts taking pictures. You keep a close eye on the herd. The big female still seems bothered that you're so close. Suddenly, she charges forward. But she stops after just a few steps.

"Don't worry, that's what they call a bluff charge," Anya explains. "She's just telling us not to come any closer."

"Are you sure she's not telling us that we're already too close?" you ask, feeling uneasy.

"Relax. Just give me a few more minutes. I want to get some good photos of the babies over there."

• To wait for Anya, turn to page 94.
• To back away now, turn to page 96.

You once read that the best way to survive a bear attack is to make yourself look big and threatening. Maybe that will work with gorillas too. You spring to your feet, spreading your arms wide and shouting at the gorilla as loudly as you can.

It was the first idea that popped into your mind. But it was a very bad one. Gorillas—especially males—are highly territorial. They respond to threats swiftly and violently, and you've just made yourself into a threat.

You can't blame the gorilla. It didn't understand that you weren't interested in its territory. It just followed its instincts to protect itself, its territory, and its troop. Unfortunately, that means a brutal and painful end to your Congo adventure.

THE END

To follow another path, turn to page 9.
To learn more about mountain survival, turn to page 99.

You shrug. Ripples could be anything. It's important to be careful in a wild place like the Congo. But you can't be afraid of every little thing. So you and Samir continue on, sloshing through the water to reach the tree.

Before you can get there, everything changes. The water suddenly churns. It almost seems to erupt, as something huge emerges. It charges straight for you. For a moment, all you see is an impossibly large mouth and long, sharp teeth—like some legendary river monster.

Then you realize the truth. This is no mythical beast. It's a hippo—probably the most dangerous and aggressive creature you could meet out here.

Samir screams. You turn to run. But you can't outrun a hippo—especially in the water. Hippos are big, but they can also be amazingly fast in short bursts. You're about to learn that lesson in the hardest way.

THE END

To follow another path, turn to page 9.
To learn more about mountain survival, turn to page 99.

You've had enough wildlife encounters for one day. You're not about to press your luck by walking up to a herd of wild elephants. "Anya, it's a bad idea. Let's just watch them from here."

Anya starts to head toward the herd anyway, but Tina stops her. "I agree, and I'm in charge here. We can watch the elephants from here. It's not worth the risk. We know what they might do."

Anya scowls, but she doesn't argue. The four of you watch the amazing creatures for almost an hour. It's fascinating to watch them interact with each other. Two young elephants stay close to their mothers—who keep an eye on you from across the distance. Finally, the herd moves on.

"Okay, back to work," Tina says. You spend another hour searching for insects before you return to camp to begin cataloging what you've found. Tomorrow you head back home. Your adventure in the Virunga Mountains will be over. But you've got memories to last a lifetime, and you wouldn't trade them for anything.

THE END

To follow another path, turn to page 9.
To learn more about mountain survival, turn to page 99.

"Well hurry up and take the pictures," you tell Anya. "I'm really not feeling good about this right now."

The female elephant's behavior quickly changes. Her ears are no longer sticking out. Now, they're tucked back. And she curls her trunk back, under her body.

"She's doing something," you say, panicking. But before Anya can reply, it happens. The elephant charges, and this time it's no bluff. The ground rumbles as she sprints at you with shocking speed. You realize too late that a female elephant will do anything to protect its young. She tried to tell you that you were making her uncomfortable, but you ignored her warnings. And so she's doing what she thinks she has to do to keep her little ones safe.

You turn to run. But it's hopeless. The elephant closes the distance in a matter of seconds. She lowers her long, curved tusks and slams them into you.

You feel a flash of pain before the world goes black. You took a big gamble in approaching a herd of wild elephants. And you lost.

THE END

To follow another path, turn to page 9.
To learn more about mountain survival, turn to page 99.

"This is no good Anya," you say. "It's not worth it. I'm going back."

You beg Anya to come with you, but she insists on taking more photos. You carefully back away, avoiding sudden movements. You just want to put as much distance between you and the herd as you can.

A minute passes. Two. The female elephant's gaze is locked on Anya. Silently, you wish for your partner to get away.

When the elephant finally charges, you're at a safe distance. But Anya isn't. You scream as you see the huge animal slam into your friend. You close your eyes, unwilling to watch. You know how this is going to end.

You managed to survive a few close encounters with some of the most fascinating creatures in Virunga National Park. But Anya was not so lucky. A dream trip has turned into a nightmare. It will haunt you for the rest of your life.

THE END

To follow another path, turn to page 9.
To learn more about mountain survival, turn to page 99.

CHAPTER 5

MOUNTAIN SURVIVAL

Mountains cover about 24 percent of Earth's land mass. They vary from low ranges, such as the Appalachian Mountains in the eastern United States, to the towering Himalayan range in Asia.

Mountains have rocky slopes, cold temperatures, and thin air at high elevations. They present a wide variety of survival challenges for the creatures that call them home. The higher you go, the more challenging the climate.

Plants and animals have developed a wide range of strategies to survive in these extreme environments. Many plants at high elevation focus on growing down—not up. They send roots deep into the mountain soil, and keep aboveground growth as small as possible.

With most of the plant underground, it's protected from the extreme weather above ground. Growing seasons are often short, so the plants need to be able to survive under snow for months at a time.

Animals face similar challenges. They stay warm with thick layers of fur. Many mountain animals have small ears and limbs to limit the loss of body heat. Some survive by hibernating for much of the year. The alpine marmot—a small mammal—can hibernate for up to nine months at a time! Mountain goats have adapted to eat just about any plant matter they can find. In a habitat with so few resources, they can't afford to be fussy.

Predators don't usually do well at very high elevations. They need a lot of energy to hunt, and there just isn't enough food available near the peaks. They often remain lower, where prey is more abundant.

Wolves, mountain lions, bears, lynx, and coyotes are just a few common mountain predators. In such harsh conditions, predators can't be picky eaters. They'll go after about any food source they can find. Few animal hunters seek out humans. But under the right conditions, any of them can be a threat to people.

SURVIVAL TIPS

Humans in the mountains face many of the same challenges that animals do. Cold temperatures, snow cover, wind, lack of resources, and thin mountain air all make survival a challenge. So how can you prepare for a mountain adventure? And what should you do if you find yourself lost or stranded in a mountain environment?

The first thing to remember is never to go into the mountains without telling someone where you'll be. That way, if something happens, people will know where to look for you.

Next, be prepared. Bring warm clothing, water, and emergency food. Tools like camping gear, a warm sleeping bag, and a compass can also be the difference between life and death.

If you're headed into an area with lots of predators, bear spray or pepper spray can be a lifesaver. A cell phone is also great—if you can get service. In most remote areas like a mountaintop, phones can't get a signal.

If you're caught unprepared, do anything you can to survive. Nights in the mountains can get very cold. Build a fire if you can. It will provide warmth and might also keep some predators away. Cover yourself with leaves, pine needles, branches, or anything else you can find. Even snow can work if you're out of options.

Finally, be prepared for wildlife encounters. Survival experts agree that most predators will keep their distance from humans when possible. Make a lot of noise as you move around. Then predators are more likely to move away. They're far more dangerous when you surprise them.

The Rispoli Family

In 2019, Elisa and Matt Rispoli, along with their two kids, were camping in Canada's Banff National Park. The family was in their tent when they got an unwelcome visitor—a wolf. Matt quickly put himself between the wolf and his family as Elisa covered the children with her body. They shouted for help—and they got it. A nearby camper, Russ Fee, heard the shouting. Fee kicked at the wolf, startling it. Both he and Matt shouted at it, sending the wolf running away. Matt had injuries from the wolf's bite, but the family made it through the ordeal alive.

Mike Vilhauer

In 2014, Mike Vilhauer got lost in California's Sierra Nevada mountains. Vilhauer had planned a day of fishing and hiking. But he lost his way. With no food or shelter, he survived five days in the rugged mountains. At night, he covered himself with pine needles and branches to keep warm. Vilhauer steered clear of dangerous wildlife and managed to survive until rescuers finally found him.

Erin McKenzie

In 2020, Erin McKenzie was out for a run with her dogs at Riding Mountain National Park in Canada when she came face-to-face with a black bear. Before she knew it, the bear whacked her across the face with its claws, tearing open her skin. As she went to the ground, the bear swiped again, this time clawing deep across her back. Bleeding and afraid, McKenzie walked 40 minutes back to her car. Her boyfriend met her there and drove her to the hospital. She was left with scars on her face and back, but it could have been much worse.

Fina Kiefer

Fina Kiefer of Alaska was hiking through the mountains in 2021 when she wandered off the trail and got lost. Kiefer tried to find her own way back. Instead, she ended up coming upon two brown bears. One of the bears charged, and Kiefer had to act quickly. An experienced hiker, she carried a can of pepper spray with her. She grabbed the can and sprayed right at the bear's face. It worked. The pepper spray turned the bear away. Afterward, Kiefer had to spend two nights alone in the wilderness. She ate snow and cranberries and started a fire. On the third day, she found a road and was rescued by someone driving by.

OTHER PATHS TO EXPLORE

This book looks at what it might be like to survive wildlife encounters in the mountains. It takes toughness, good decision-making, and a little bit of luck to make it through the most dangerous situations. How might others survive in the mountains?

1) From ancient times to the modern day, people have made the mountains their home. How might survival have been different 1,000 or even 100 years ago? How would people from the past have survived without modern technology?

2) Sometimes, people lost in the mountains need rescue. But the people who go look for them face dangers too. Cold weather, avalanches, and wildlife are a threat to rescuers. If you were a rescuer, how would you feel? What clues would you look for when searching for someone who is lost?

3) Mountains are just one place where people can have a dangerous wildlife encounter. In what other environments might you come face-to-face with a deadly animal? How might survival strategies differ in places such as the desert or at sea?

GLOSSARY

adapt (uh-DAPT)—to change in order to survive

antivenom (an-tee-VE-nuhm)—a medicine that helps the body fight off the effects of animal venom

catalog (KAT-uh-log)—to record a number of items

epinephrine (eh-puh-NEH-frin)—a medicine that helps counter the effects of an allergic reaction

forage (FOR-ij)—to search for food in the wilderness

habitat (HAB-uh-tat)—the natural place and conditions in which a plant or animal lives

hibernate (HYE-bur-nate)—to spend the winter in a dormant, sleeplike state to save energy

predator (PRED-uh-tur)—an animal that hunts other animals for food

prey (PRAY)—an animal hunted by other animals as food

primate (PRYE-mate)—one of a group of intelligent animals that includes humans, apes, and monkeys

territorial (TER-uh-tor-ee-uhl)—protective of one's home

BIBLIOGRAPHY

Davies, Barry. *SAS Mountain & Arctic Survival.* New York: Simon & Schuster, 2012.

Eckhart, Gene and Annette Lanjouw. *Mountain Gorillas: Biology, Conservation, and Coexistence.* Baltimore: Johns Hopkins University Press, 2009.

Elbroch, Mark. *The Cougar Conundrum: Sharing the World with a Successful Predator.* Washington, DC: Island Press, 2020.

Herrero, Stephen. *Bear Attacks: Their Causes and Avoidance.* Guilford, CT: Rowman & Littlefield, 2018.

Snakebites: First Aid mayoclinic.org/first-aid/first-aid-snake-bites/basics/art-20056681

READ MORE

Doeden, Matt. *Can You Survive Dangerous Desert Encounters?* North Mankato, MN: Capstone Press, 2022.

O'Brien, Cynthia. *Mountain Survival Guide.* New York: Crabtree Publishing Company, 2021.

Sommer, Nathan. *Grizzly Bear vs. Wolf Pack.* Minneapolis: Bellwether Media, 2020.

INTERNET SITES

How Can I Survive a Night in the Alaskan Wilderness?
adventure.howstuffworks.com/survive-night-alaska.htm

Mountain Habitat
kids.nationalgeographic.com/nature/habitats/article/mountain

Mountain Range Geography
ducksters.com/geography/mountain_ranges.php

ABOUT THE AUTHOR

Matt Doeden is a freelance author and editor from Minnesota. He's written numerous children's books on sports, music, current events, the military, extreme survival, and much more. His books *Sandy Koufax* (Twenty-First Century Books, 2006) and *Tom Brady: Unlikely Champion* (Twenty-First Century Books, 2011) were Junior Library Guild selections. Matt began his career as a sportswriter before turning to publishing. He lives in Minnesota with his wife and two children.

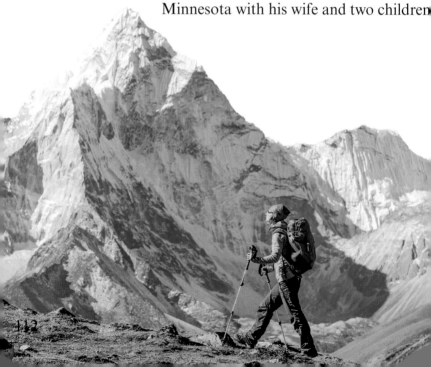